# THE WARSAW GHETTO
# 1940-1945

On the fifth aniversary of the Ghetto rising, April 19, 1948 a monument presenting the heroes of the Ghetto, the work of Natan Rappaport, was unveiled. The photograph shows a fragment of the monument.

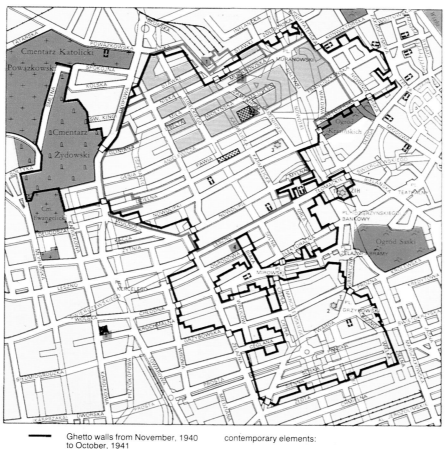

| | |
|---|---|
| ▬ | Ghetto walls from November, 1940 to October, 1941 |
| ☐ | Ghetto gates |
| ▬ | Ghetto walls during August, 1942 |
| ▨ | Ghetto area from September, 1942 to April, 1943 |
| CIEPŁA | the then existing street network |
| ⛪ | synagogues: 1 – Great, 2 – Nożyk, 3 – Morij |
| ■ | orphanage, managed by J. Korczak until 1940 |
| ▨ | prison |

contemporary elements:

| | |
|---|---|
| PROSTA | the contemporary street network |

places of remembrance:

| | |
|---|---|
| 1 | the Umschlag-platz Monument |
| 2 | the Hereos of the Ghetto Memorial Monument |
| 3 | slab commemorating the Jewish Combat Organization bunker site |
| 4 | plaque marking the building lived in by I. Lewartowski |
| 5 | the J. Korczak Monument |
| T | the E. R. Kaminska Jewish Theater |
| HI | the Jewish Historical Institute |

# THE WARSAW GHETTO

# THE WARSAW GHETTO
## RUTA SAKOWSKA

In the years 1918-39 Warsaw represented the largest concentration of Jews in Europe, and the second largest (after New York) in the world. On the eve of the Second World War, its population included c. 380,000 Jews, or almost 30% of the total population.

The Warsaw ghetto, which the occupying forces cut off from the rest of the city during the night from November 15th to 16th, 1940, contained in the period of the greatest congestion (spring 1941) c. 450,000 inhabitants, crammed into the relatively small area of c. 307 hectares.

The number of Jews in occupied Warsaw rose as a result of compulsory re-settlement, primarily from the Polish territories which had been absorbed into the Reich and those which formed what was termed the Warsaw District. The number however rapidly decreased as a result of the exceptionally high death rate in this sealed area (898 deaths in January 1941 and 5,560 in January 1942 – a nearly six-fold increase!). In all from October 1939 to mid-1942, c. 100,000 Jews died in Warsaw, chiefly from starvation and epidemic diseases.

Both slow death from hunger and violent death in the gas chambers were products of Nazi policy of direct and indirect extermination. The basic forms of indirect extermination were plunder, slave labour, and the gradual elimination of Jews from socio-economic life, followed by their concentration in isolated districts; direct extermination took the form of the total annihilation of concentrations of Jewish population.

The first stage ended definitively after 22 months of Nazi occupation; the first mass executions of Jews in the summer of 1941 in the territories newly occupied after the invasion of the USSR, marked the beginning of the second stage. In Warsaw the first annihilation campaign began on July 22nd and by September 21st, 1942, absorbed some 300,000 victims, who were murdered in Treblinka.

With the escalation of Nazi extermination activities, the forms of self-defence, counter-action and resistance of the Jewish population also changed. This evolution can be detected particularly clearly in Warsaw. During the period of indirect extermination, the community enclosed in the district exhibited enormous resistance to the destructive activities of the occupying power, and fought desperately for existence. This struggle was not however fought in the open, but in the underground current of community life.

In the sealed Jewish districts, processes analogous to those taking place on the other side of the wall could be seen. On both sides of the wall, underneath the surface of life under occupation – that „make-believe life", if I might make use of the title of Kazimierz Wyka's wellknown book – an authentic life, which escaped the control of the occupying authorities, managed to break through.

Economic activity developed in the ghetto underground, and this caused a fundamental breach in the Nazi system of isolation and limitations. Nazi prohibitions were broken on both sides of the wall, for otherwise life was impossible. Insubordination was universal.

In the Warsaw ghetto, civil resistance, inspired or indeed directly led in conspiracy, concentrated primarily on the battle against hunger. Although the forms and methods employed in this battle were varied and legion, they can be reduced basically to two inseparable elements: the first was material assistance, and the second defence against psychic deformation – a dramatic fight to preserve values, both in the sphere of human relations, and that of spiritual needs. It was a kind of recovery of their personality by people who had been pushed by the occupying power to the very depths of poverty and humiliation.

## VOLUNTARY MUTUAL AID

In view of the universal threat, the primary task of the underground movement in the ghetto was to unite the community behind the most important aim, which was to save the starving. Apart from the Judenrats, the openly-operating institutions in the ghettos of the Generalgouvernement (General Government) were the Jewish Voluntary Mutual Aid Organizations. Under their banner, a network of social aid organizations sprang up: as well as the pre-war voluntary organizations (for example, Centos, the Society for Care of Orphans and Abandoned Children; TOZ, the Society for the Protection of Health, and so on), new forms were set up during the years of war and occupation, functioning on the basis of neighbourly ties. These were the Warsaw house committees and the local confraternities formed by the re-settled populations.

Fundamental changes occurred in the social links in neighbourly micro-societies. Life forced them to overcome the phenomenon of big-city isolation, with its patterns of indifference and formality in inter-human contacts. The germs of solidarity and mutual assistance showed strong signs of life, and gave rise to an active approach to suffering. Even pauperized families shared what they had with the starving (a crust of bread or a carrot was a gift that counted for something), doctors treated the children of their neighbours free of charge, cobblers repaired boots free of charge, and so on.

The thousands of house committees in the ghetto gave rise to numerous commissions and to ladies' circles, youth circles, children's groups, etc. Sometimes a house in the ghetto could hold from several hundred to a thousand inhabitants. These were compact complexes of buildings surrounding one (or sometimes two or three) of the deep well courtyards that were typical of pre-war Warsaw; they formed separate housing sectors with a gate that was closed long before the curfew, and gradually became not only self-sufficient centres of neighbourly assistance, education, social life, cultural and religious life, but also links in a chain of tenant selfadministration that were recognized even by the occupying power.

These instances of voluntary mutual help provided a cover for the conspiratorial organizations of the ghetto underground.

## UNDERGROUND CULTURE

Alongside material assistance, underground culture became the second most important element in civil resistance in the ghetto.

The desperate, unequal struggle for existence by no means obscured the spiritual needs of the ghetto's inhabitants, for life confirmed the significance of spiritual needs in the fight for individual and collective survival.

As was the case throughout the whole country, new forms of underground culture, which evaded the control of the occupying forces, began to take shape from the first days of the occupation. These were admittedly based on primitive means of communication, but nonetheless became predominant in the life of the community: secret teaching at elementary, secondary and higher level, secret musical performances, secret religious activity, underground literary publications and journalism (in 1940-42 more than 40 titles appeared in the underground press, mainly in Yiddish and Polish), secret academic research in history, sociology, ethnography, medicine (starvation-related illnesses); there were also secret libraries that supplied books to their readers' homes. The book trade moved out of the closed-down bookshops into the streets. Leopold Staff wrote (1927):

*More than bread*
*Poetry is necessary at times*
*When there's no need for it at all...*

These words of an outstanding poet, which were quoted in the text of an invitation to a literary evening in the ghetto in February 1942, could be taken as the leading theme for cultural life in the whole of occupied Poland.

Underground culture took shape as a fighting culture. It was the underground movement that was the patron and inspiration for cultural life, as for other forms of civil resistance. The underground made available to people working in the arts their channels of information and their media of communication; it made use of the work of historians, writers, journalists, psychologists, teachers, actors and musicians, who published their work in the underground press, edited reports on underground activities, wrote proclamations and songs, worked in the underground education movement, etc. The underground also extended its patronage to the secret current of religious life. The young conspirators, who were to be the fighters of the Jewish Fighting Organization (ŻOB), worked in the youth circles attached to the house committees and in the underground education movement. Often they played a double role: as a pupil in the underground secondary school groups, and then as a teacher of younger children. Young people played the greatest, if not the decisive, role in editing, printing and distributing the underground press.

In cultural life, as in other areas of the life of the community, the links between the ghetto and the „Aryan side" were not broken. A Polish doctor, Professor Franciszek Raszeja, paid for these contacts with his life: he was shot by the Nazis during a visit to a patient in the ghetto. Irena Sedler, a Polish woman who was an active member of the Council for Aid to Jews, used to enter the ghetto on the business of voluntary mutual aid, and she sometimes attended secret literary and musical performances organized by the youth circles, where the works of Chopin were played and the poetry of Broniewski was read.

The Polish underground press and secret editions of literary works were also smuggled into the ghetto and circulated in the form of copies among the young people. There were also links that were not made actual: the yearning of the Varsovians of the sealed district for their city, that „sentimental smuggling" that Władysław Szlengel wrote about.

## THE UNDERGROUND GHETTO ARCHIVE (ARG)

Accounts of the fate of Jews from almost all the occupied country came into this centre, and the information in them was analyzed here; reports on Nazi genocide were sent out from here into the world.

The founder of and inspiration behind the ARG was Emmanuel Ringelblum (1900-44), a historian, an active figure in public life, a journalist and teacher.

The origin of the archive lay in the Notes, a chronicle compiled by Ringelblum from September 1939. In the autumn of 1940, an underground archival-documentary centre with the cryptonym of Oneg Shabat (literally in Hebrew, „joy", „Sabbath pleasure", but in this sense rather „Sabbath meeting") was set up on his initiative. The bulletins issued by this centre, intended for the Polish underground press, were signed ARG (Ghetto Archive).

Oneg Shabat was a group of a dozen or more permanent co-workers. The first secretary of the group was a young economist, Hersz Wasser, who was responsible in the ARG for the section dealing with accounts from ghettos outside Warsaw; he kept records of materials and authors. In the organizational and technical sense the underground Archive was his creation; his wife, Bluma, actively assisted him. The other secretary was Eliahu Gutkowski, a teacher, writer, and popularizer of science, who took an active part in political life. Those who worked with the ARG, or sent their texts there, included writers such as Icchak Kacenelson and Janusz Korczak, rabbis (for example one of the closest associates of Ringelblum, the self-taught historian, Szymon Huberband), and academics, like the economist Menachem Linder. The majority of those who worked with or wrote for the ARG belonged to underground organizations (including Mordechaj Anielewicz).

The people associated with the ARG intended in the future to piece together the history of the Jews in occupied Poland – that is, contemporary history. The nature of the research therefore dictated the application of sociological methods. The materials of the ARG were created and collected on the basis of a much-discussed questionnaire. Draft plans for works of synthesis have also survived, along with arguments for specific issues and guide questions for members of the group, addressed to various generational and professional groups, for example, to children, young people, booksellers, librarians, barbers, artists, members of the Jewish Council, etc.

The materials of the ARG fall into thematic and chronological cycles. The themes were dictated by life under the occupation.

Widely varying materials were collected in the underground Archive. These included official documents (proclamations, copies of official correspondence, etc.), and also personal documents (diaries, letters, etc.), and even advertising hand-outs, medical prescriptions and the wrapping papers from sweets produced in the ghetto. Education is well-represented (including school reports, children's essays, etc.) as is cultural life (posters, invitations to literary events, concerts, etc.). A considerable amount of material on the underground organizations which later formed the ŻOB has also been collected. There are therefore notes on allied radio broadcasts, which were later published in the underground press, programme documents, appeals, and also all-Polish materials from underground seminars for youth organizations which took place in the Warsaw ghetto.

The largest collection in the materials, that of the underground press with more than 40 titles representing various factions, is also of the greatest importance.

## TWO GENERATIONS.
## THE INFORMAL SELF-ADMINISTRATION

Tens of thousands of people took part in the battle against hunger. These included both those who had been active in public life before the war and also the „new ones" (including a significant number of women). These were believers and non-believers, young and old – and among the youngest were the future members of the ŻOB which was to become the main force in the uprising in the Warsaw ghetto.

At the time of the uprising (1943) the majority of the members of the ŻOB were between 20 and 24 years of age, and so in the first period of the occupation they were nearly four years younger. In the period of indirect extermination therefore, an older generation composed of those in their forties and fifties created the climate of life in the community. The organizers of the civil resistance movement were adults: the leaders and active members of political parties. These activities were directed by a group of political party leaders, representing various points on the political spectrum: from the Orthodox religious Agudas Israel, through the Zionist and socialist Zionist parties, to the socialist Bund and (from January 1942) the newly created Polish Workers' Party (PPR), ghetto branch.

The phenomenon whereby important socio-organizational functions were taken over by informal groups, which could be observed throughout the occupied country, also occurred in the sealed Jewish districts. In the battle for life of the starving, it was in the centres for voluntary self-help, which officially limited themselves to charitable activities, that the authentic if informal self-government of the ghetto took shape. The tip of this structure was the conspiratorial group of political party leaders, while the base was provided by more than a thousand house committees.

# EVOLUTION OF FORMS OF RESISTANCE

The evolution of forms of resistance took place in an atmosphere of generational conflict. The idea of armed resistance took shape among the young people of the underground, who were growing up quickly in the conditions of the war and occupation. An analysis of texts in the underground ghetto newspapers shows that this idea was not completely foreign to the future members of the ŻOB from the first years of the occupation. It was initially a concept or rather a vision (in the belief that conflict between Nazi Germany and the USSR was inevitable), of armed activity by Jewish young people at the time when the front was approaching, alongside the victorious allies, shoulder to shoulder with the Red Army, fighting side by side with Poles and other nations struggling for their national independence.

Visions of the status of the Jews in the post-war world freed of the Nazis which can be found in the texts of the underground newspapers of the ghetto, varied according to political orientation, but at their base was a hope – perfectly justified in the light of experience to date – of surviving the war, of Jews being present in a better post-war world, and in a liberated and democratic Poland. But all the visions – that of being present in a Berlin liberated by the victorious allies, among the crowds carrying portraits of Marx and Lenin, that of a happy spring after the pulling down of the ghetto walls, of a future in Palestine, of a free democratic Poland and of taking part in a post-war peace conference – proved illusory for the people of the ghetto.

# NEWS OF EXTERMINATION

The occupying power had started on the elimination of concentrations of Jewish population in the second half of 1941 in the territories newly occupied after the invasion of the Soviet Union. In December 1941, the first extermination centre in Polish territory was set up at Chełmno-on-the-Ner, in the region known as the Wartheland. In the spring and summer of 1942, three further extermination centres were set up in the General Government: at Bełżec, Sobibor and Treblinka. Auschwitz became a mass extermination centre.

Members of the underground in the Warsaw ghetto carefully recorded signals about the extermination of other ghettos. The collection, checking and analysis of the information was the task of the ARG.

The accounts of witnesses – those who escaped from places where an annihilation campaign had been carried out, and who when they arrived in Warsaw reported to the delegates of their compatriots' organizations – were of the greatest significance.

The reports of the underground couriers were particularly valuable since, under false names, they managed to travel almost the length and breadth of the occupied country. These were usually girls with light-coloured hair, that is, as is was said, of Aryan appearance, who were elegant, knew foreign languages, and were not afraid to make social conversation. They boldly made their way through the police cordons at railway stations, sometimes in the company of charming German travelling companions who were helping them to carry their heavy cases, full of literature. One of these girls was „Lonka" Koziebrodzka, before the war a student of Romance languages at Warsaw University, who was a correspondent of the ARG. But on dangerous missions, the most important quality in a courier was courage and quick thinking. „Frumka", as she was known familiarly, one of the legendary Płotnicka sisters, who was darkhaired and Semitic in appearance, managed to get through everywhere, where others had not managed.

Post-cards coming into the Warsaw ghetto were also a major source of information (this was the only form of correspondence allowed by the Germans to the residents of the ghetto). Although at the beginning of the extermination campaign, the Sipo introduced a Postsperre (ban on postal services) in many towns, nonetheless, post-cards from places threatened with liquidation reached the Warsaw ghetto relatively quickly, within four or five days. The people at the ARG placed a great deal of importance on these letters: they were collected, copies were made, and some of them were published in the underground press.

It is possible to re-create the circulation of information about the course of extermination from the underground press, personal accounts and letters with a post-mark.

The first news of the Nazi massacres of the Jewish population in the territories newly occupied after the attack on the USSR appeared in the underground press at the end of September and the beginning of October 1941.

Shortly, alarming news began to reach the Warsaw ghetto from the opposite, western side of occupied Poland. Unbelievable rumours began to circulate about transports of Jews which disappeared without trace in the palace at Chełmno-on-the-Ner, which was occupied by the SS. The Judenrats from nearby small towns sent envoys to reconnoitre, and the neighbouring peasants spoke about what was happening in whispers; one of them, Stanisław Kaszyński of Chełmno, was shot in

February 1942 for spreading information about the extermination centre. On January 19th, 1942, three escapees from the Chełmno death camp reached nearby Grabów: they had been eye-witnesses of the mass killing of Jews and Gypsies in gas-lorries. The tales of the escapees gave rise to a spate of letters to families in the Warsaw ghetto. One advance signal of a coming liquidation campaign in many small towns was the imposition of a poll tax of 4 to 8 Marks. Where this „demonic" tax – as it was termed by the ARG – was announced, people wrote letters of farewell.

It was the post-cards that began to arrive from the beginning of January 1942 from Grabów, Kutno, Krośniewice, Gostynin and Gąbin that brought the first news of the death centre at Chełmno-on-the-Ner.

Shortly thereafter, one of the escapees from Chełmno, „Szlamek", reached the Warsaw ghetto. „Szlamek's" account made the rounds of the underground press.

As the Nazi extermination activities escalated, the wave of blood was drawing ever nearer to Warsaw.

The third warning was the news which arrived in mid-March 1942, of the murder of the Jewish population of Lublin – and this was now within the boundaries of the General Government, barely 150 km. distant from Warsaw. Almost simultaneously came reports of a liquidation campaign in Lvov, carried out in March and April 1942.

## RAISING THE ALARM ABOUT NAZI CRIMES

In the spring of 1942, under the impact of news about fresh and dangerous forms of extermination of the Jews now being practiced, the ARG group began a second important programme, alongside their long-term research work: they started to work to alarm public opinion about the Nazi genocide.

A special information service was set up, and Polish secret organizations were alerted.

The underground press of the Warsaw ghetto published information about the extermination campaign. At the same time, the Home Army intelligence service was collecting data on Nazi genocide. The ARG reports were sent abroad through the mediacy of the Department for Jewish Affairs of the High Command of the Home Army, which was under the direction of Henryk Woliński: these reports dealt with Chełmno in March 1942, the liquidation campaign in the Lublin region in April 1942, and the massacres in other ghettos in July 1942.

The activities of the ARG did not pass unnoticed. At the end of April 1942, an article entitled „The Jews" appeared in the underground Biuletyn Informacyjny (Information Bulletin) published by the High Command of the Home Army. This sounded the alarm on the extinction of the inhabitants of the Warsaw ghetto, the mass executions in the Eastern territories, the extermination centre at Chełmno-on-the-Ner and what were termed the „re-settlements" from Lublin and the small towns of the Lublin region. The author of the article made use of the testimony of the escapees from Chełmno: „The accounts by eye-witnesses of the murders perpetrated at Chełmno with the help of poison gas, prove that the Germans have surpassed themselves."

The Nazi campaign to exterminate the Jews evoked a wave of protests in the Polish underground press. Publicity was also given to the matter abroad (although too late, in Ringelblum's view). On June 26th, 1942, Radio London, which had been giving news about the extermination of the Jews for several weeks, broadcast a major programme, based partly on the ARG reports, on the Nazi extermination of Jews in Poland. In connection with this programme, Emmanuel Ringelblum noted, „In alarming the world about our plight, the Oneg Shabat group has fulfilled a great historic mission. This may perhaps save hundreds of thousands of Polish Jews. This will become clear in the nearest future. I don't know who from our group will remain alive, who will be permitted by fate to work on the materials we have collected, but we can be certain of one thing – that our sacrifices, risks and the tension of constant danger, our labours and sufferings, have not been in vain."

## THE CONCEPT OF ARMED STRUGGLE

The news about the extermination speeded up the consolidation of the concept of armed struggle. In the spring of 1942, news reached the Warsaw ghetto of the armed self-defence of Jews at Nowogródek in the Vilna region. The news moved the young people of the underground. In the underground newspapers we can read that Nowogródek had become „a symbol of the struggle for respect of human life, which rejects the idea of resignation and despair. May Nowogródek be a pattern for a dignified human attitude".

Post-war research has not been able to establish whether the self-defence of Nowogródek did in fact really take place -whether it was an historical fact or an heroic legend. In the opinion of the outstanding historian of this period, Israel Gutman of Yad Vashem, no official sources contain mention of this revolt. Nor do we know how news of it reached

Warsaw. Nonetheless, the news from Nowogródek fascinated the young people of the ghetto underground.

At this point, a small digression: after the war the stereotype became generally accepted of the „fight for honour", or, as it is sometimes termed in a slightly more acceptable form, the fight for human dignity, as the primary or indeed only motivating factor for the ghetto fighters. Here we can read between the lines a subtext which contrasts, perhaps not entirely consciously, „two kinds of death": „beautiful" or „dignified" death in battle, and the other kind, by execution or in gas fumes. Is it possible that the innocent victims have lost, as Antoni Słonimski wrote, not only life but also honour and glory?

It is therefore worth considering the meaning of the words about „a dignified attitude" and a „dignified death" in the underground ghetto press. These words in no way indicate a choice of a „more beautiful" way of dying, nor do they imply condemnation of the hundreds and thousands of defenceless victims who were „led to the slaughter" and died without a struggle. The fragments of texts quoted show that for the future insurrectionaries of the ghetto, the slogan „to die with honour" meant to make the sacrifice of their death and in this way confirm the value of human life which in the case of the Jewish population was destroyed by the Nazis so easily – and what was particularly painful – with impunity and without their own casualties.

Armed struggle became almost an obsession with the young people of the underground, especially those belonging to the Hechalutz movement. One of the leading girl soldiers of the ghetto, and the co-founder of the ŻOB, Cywia Lubetkin, was to write years later in her memoirs, „Before us was the enormous power of a victorious army. One great state after another was capitulating before it. „ What could these boys and girls from the sealed Jewish district, this handful of what seemed to be dreamers, put up against the might of Third Reich?".

Initially, the adults, the political party leaders, treated the young people with some reserve, warning them against premature action, and pointing to the collective responsibility of the population of the ghetto. In this situation, the only realistic chance for fighting the occupying forces was partisan warfare in the woods. This was the idea of the PPR, newly formed in January 1942, which promptly made contacts with the ghetto.

At the end of March and the beginning of April 1942, the ghetto underground began to take steps to consolidate its forces and set up an armed organization. On the initiative of the PPR, an agreement was concluded in the ghetto between the political parties and youth organizations, known as the Anti-Fascist Bloc. This contained representatives of the PPR, the socialist Zionist parties and also youth organizations. At this stage the socialist Bund did not yet join the alliance. The Anti-Fascist Bloc, which created the para-military Fighting Organization represented the view that the Jews should be brought into the general partisan struggle outside the ghetto. But the liquidation campaign was relentlessly drawing nearer, and this would overrule these plans.

## THE FIRST LIQUIDATION CAMPAIGN

From July 22nd to September 21st, 1942, the Nazis murdered about 300,000 people from the Warsaw ghetto at Treblinka. In this period, the underground did not manage to organize armed resistance. The defenceless mass of civilians, with a preponderance of women, children and old people, could not raise opposition to the Nazi death machine. There seemed no prospects at this time either in the military or psychological sense for a demonstration of armed strength. We should however take note of acts of civil resistance which were of lasting significance going beyond the chronological framework of the war and Nazi occupation: on July 23rd, 1942, the chairman of the Warsaw Judenrat, Adam Czerniakow, took his own life. He saw this as the only method available to him of avoiding participation in the deportation of Jews to Treblinka. On August 5th or 6th, 1942, Janusz Korczak gave up his chance to save himself, and went to his death along with the workers and children of his orphanage.

## EPILOGUE

In what was called the Residual Ghetto (Restgetto), barely 60,000 people were left. The last months of the history of the concentration of Jewish population in Warsaw were marked by feverish preparation for the struggle. No one could now doubt that the ghetto was condemned, and the guilt connected with collective responsibility was therefore removed; the inhabitants of the ghetto no longer entertained illusions about being saved by work. Orphaned, and thrown into despair by the loss of their loved ones, they supported the future fighters.

The idea of armed combat was also supported in this period by the leaders of the political parties. Contact was made with the High Command of the AK, and also, unknown to the AK, with the PPR. The main underground forces in the ghetto were united. The Bund now joined the pact called the Jewish National Committee (ŻKN) which had been formed in the autumn of 1942, and consisted of the PPR (ghetto branch) and the liberal socialist Zionist parties together with the youth organizations. In the night from December 1st to 2nd, 1942, the statutes were passed of the Jewish Coordinating Committee (ŻKK) between the Jewish National Committee (ŻKN), the Bund, and the Jewish Fighting Organization (ŻOB). The idea of armed struggle was also put forward by the Jewish Military Union (ŻZW), which was composed mainly of right-wing Zionists, known as revisionists, whose members included a group of Polish Army reserve officers.

Let us look a little more closely at the people belonging to the ŻOB, which provided the main force behind the uprising in the Warsaw ghetto and armed actions in other ghettos. The materials at our disposal are the biographies of 235 members of the ŻOB, who died in the Warsaw ghetto or were delegated from Warsaw to other ghettos. These biographical sketches were prepared by the Israeli author Mejlech Neustadt on the basis of information given by those fighters who survived (only a dozen or so of the participants in the ghetto uprising survived the war and occupation). This information was then checked by other research workers. According to the Israeli researcher Professor Israel Gutman there were 500 members of the ŻOB and 250 members of the ŻZW. Thus the 235 biographies available form c. 50% of the total membership of the ŻOB.

The ŻOB in Warsaw was made up of 22 fighting groups, including 14 Hechalutz groups (of pioneers, preparing for the future colonization of Palestine) and allied parties: Poale-Zion Left and what was known as Poale-Zion Right; the PPR and the Bund had four fighting groups each.

The commanding officer of the ŻOB was Mordechaj Anielewicz, 24 years old and a member of the Hashomer Hatzair (in Hebrew, meaning „Young Guard") Hechalutz organization. His deputy on the „Aryan side" was Icchak Cukierman, pseudonym „Antek", a member of the Hechalutz Dror (in Hebrew, „Liberty"), who replaced „Jurek"-Arie Wilner, the arrested liaison officer with the AK; members of the central command were Marek Edelman of the Bund; Jochanan Morgensztern of Poale-Zion Right; Hersz Berliński from Poale-Zion Left; and Michał Rojzenfeld from the PPR.

Of the 235 members on which there is information, we know the age of 182; the majority (135) were born in the years 1916-23. The largest number born in a single year came in 1923: 27 persons.

These were therefore mainly very young people, who during the uprising were twenty, twenty-four, twenty-six years old. The oldest ŻOB member, Abram Diamant (Poale-Zion Left), was born in 1900 (he died in the uprising, in the battle within the ghetto, in May 1943); the youngest, Eliezer („Lusiek") Błones (Bund), was born in 1930 (he died after leaving the ghetto through the sewers, on the „Aryan side").

Of the 22 group commanders of the fighting groups, 15were born in the years 1916 to 1923. The oldest was Hersz Berliński, born in 1908 (he died in the Warsaw uprising in 1944); the youngest was Dawid Hochberg (Bund), born in 1925 (he died in the first days of the ghetto uprising).

The commanding, officer of the ŻOB, Mordechaj Anielewicz, was born in 1919 (he committed suicide together with the whole command of the organization on May 8th, 1943, in the command bunker at 18 Miła Street which had been surrounded by the Nazis and filled with poison gas).

The survivors were Icchak Cukierman (Dror), born in 1915, who died in Israel in 1981; his wife, Cywia Lubetkin (Dror), born in 1918, who died in 1978; and Marek Edelman (Bund), born in 1924, who lives in Łódź.

We know the social origins of 118 of the 235. The majority came from working families: workers, craftsmen, small shop-keepers. From childhood, these young people had known poverty. Nonetheless, the group investigated also included a considerable number (at least 46) who came from wealthy bourgeois families. These included the sons and daughters of factory-owners, rich merchants, etc. „Jurek"-Arie Wilner, the famous ŻOB liaison courier with the AK, was the son of a Warsaw tannery owner (he was born in 1917, and was the initiator of the mass suicide in the ŻOB command bunker at 18 Miła Street).

Josef Joszua Winogron (Hashomer Hatzair), the leader of a fighting group (born in 1923, died during the uprising, fighting within the ghetto) was the son of a lift manufacturer; Margolit Landau (Hashomer Hatzair), who took part in the assassination of the Jewish Police Commandant, Jakub Lejkin, was the daughter of a furniture manufacturer (she was born in 1926, and died in the first self-defence of the ghetto in January 1943); her father, Aleksander Landau, who remained on the board of his firm after it had been taken over by the German firm of Ostdeutsche Bautischlerei-Werkstätte, and was an outstanding worker in the underground resistance, who sheltered members of the ŻOB in the factory premises, died in Auschwitz in 1944.

The legendary couriers, the sisters Chana („Chancia") and Fruma („Frumka") Płotnicka (Dror), were the daughters of a wealthy merchant from Płotnica near Pińsk.

However, some of these children from wealthy homes had left their families and maintained themselves by their own work already before the war – for example Arie Wilner. The members of the Hechalutz organization took part in „hakchshara" (professional preparation for physical work), in youth communes known as kibbutzim; these also existed in the Warsaw ghetto.

During the years of the occupation, the majority  earned their own living, and for the most part as manual workers. A considerable number of the future members of the ŻOB worked in the youth farms outside the territory of the ghetto at Grochów and Czerniaków. Nor did the members of the ŻOB avoid compulsory labour camps.

The majority of the members of the ŻOB investigated had received elementary education, but there was a considerable proportion who had received further education. The group included at least 52 people (22%) who at the end of 1939, that is at the moment when the occupation authorities closed down secondary schools and institutions of higher education throughout the occupied country, were pupils in or graduates of secondary schools, or were receiving or had graduated from higher education. The largest group was formed by pupils at or graduates of secondary grammar schools (at least 38). On the whole, they had attended renowned Jewish private schools in Warsaw which taught in the medium of Polish, like the boys' Laor Grammar School (in Hebrew, „to the light"; Mordechaj Anielewicz, the commanding officer of the ŻOB, had attended this school); the boys' Askola (Haskalah) Grammar School (in Hebrew, „Enlightenment"), or the Girls' Yehudiya Grammar School.

The members of the ŻOB also included people who had attended schools outside Warsaw: for example Tosia Altman of the Hashomer Hatzair attended the Hebrew Grammar School at Włocławek; she was born in 1918, was a ŻOB courier, and was one of the 14 who remained alive in the command bunker at 18 Miła Street; she was taken out through the sewers onto the „Aryan side" on May 10th, 1943, badly burned from the fire in a ŻOB hide-out at 11 Listopada Street, and was arrested and tortured to death by the Gestapo at the end of May 1943.

There were at least a few students in the group investigated. These included Lea („Lonka") Koziebrodzka, a student of Romance languages at the University of Warsaw, born in 1917, and arrested in 1942; she died in Auschwitz as a Polish woman, Krystyna Kosowska, in March 1943.

Mordechaj Tenenbaum („Tamaroff"; of the Dror) was a student in the Oriental Studies department at the University of Warsaw; he was delegated to Białystok by the ŻOB, and was one of the commanders of the uprising in the ghetto there; he was born in 1916, and died after the uprising had been broken in August 1943.

The psychologist Michał Rojzenfeld of the PPR, a member of the high command of the ŻOB, was either a student or graduate of the University of Warsaw; he was born in 1916, and died in partisan fighting in the Wyszków forest in the summer of 1943.

Only a few of the older members of the ŻOB are definitely known to have managed to complete their studies before the war. Abram Blum („Abrasha"), a leading activist of the Bund, was a graduate of the Polytechnic in Ghent; he was born in 1904, was the organizer of the workers' battalions during the defence of Warsaw in September 1939; a member of a fighting group of the Bund; reached the „Aryan side" through the sewers, where he died as a result of being handed over to the Nazis by an informer. Edward Fondamiński of the PPR was a graduate of the Polytechnic of Warsaw; he was born in 1916, and died together with his wife Luba in the ŻOB command bunker at 18 Miła Street.

The members of the ŻOB investigated included 71 women (c. 30%). The image of these girls, who bore arms and fought alongside the men, was immortalized in his report by the butcher of the ghetto, General JŘrgen Stroop.

There were many cases where families fought together in the ŻOB: these were mainly brothers and sisters, or young married couples. For example, we know already of Chana and Fruma Płotnicka; their brother, Hersz, also died fighting against the occupying forces. The sisters Basia and Sara Sylman (born in 1925 and 1926) came to Warsaw with a Dror group from Ostrowiec Kielecki at the end of 1942, after the liquidation campaign in that ghetto. 17-year-old Sara („Sujka") died in the first self-defence action in the ghetto in January 1943, and her elder sister Basia in May 1943. The whole Błones family fought in the ghetto uprising: Jurek, Guta and Lusiek. After they escaped from the burning ghetto through the sewers on May 10th, 1943, they were murdered by the Nazis in the village of Płudy, near Łomianki, in the vicinity of Warsaw.

Love played a great role in the lives of these young people from the underground. We can find at least a dozen married couples among the members of the ŻOB. With only a few exceptions, these were not legalized unions, but were completely accepted among the young people, and were noted in the literature.

The fighting families were usually single generation families. At the time of the uprising, their parents were already dead. They had died, with very few exceptions, during the first and second liquidation campaigns in the Warsaw ghetto (July 22nd to September 21st, 1942 and January 18th to 22nd, 1943), or in other ghettos.

A feeling of being orphaned, that terrible emptiness that follows the loss of loved ones, and a helpless hatred that consumed them for the perpetrators of these misfortunes – these were important components of the emotional climate in the residual ghettos. This feeling was expressed both in the folk art and the literature of the period, and was a powerful motive force for action, the source of the inner imperative that forced them to take up the unequal struggle with the occupying forces that in military terms they lost.

From January 18th to 22nd, 1943, the ŻOB fought its first battle with the Nazis; on April 19th of the same year the uprising broke out in the Warsaw ghetto.

The fate of the ŻOB fighters reflects the history of the armed conflict in the Warsaw ghetto. Six of the 235 investigated were arrested by the Gestapo before the fighting in the ghetto. Twelve died in the autumn of 1942 in connection with an attempt to organize a partisan unit at Werbkowice near Hrubieszów. Nineteen were killed during the first self-defence action from January 18th to 22nd, 1943. Eighteen committed suicide in the ŻOB command bunker at 18 Miła Street; 69 died in the fighting in the ghetto in April to May 1943, and 28 died in the sewers. Forty-four fighters got through to the „Aryan side", mainly through the sewers. The majority of these were killed in partisan fighting in the Wyszków forest; they also died in the armed uprisings in the Białystok, Częstochowa and Będzin ghettos; three died in the Warsaw uprising. In 33 cases the circumstances of death are unknown: they died in the ghetto, or in the sewers.

During the days of the uprising, political differences ceased to have any meaning. Members of the ŻZW fought bravely and sacrificially alongside the ŻOB.

Despite their overwhelming military superiority, the Nazis, taken by surprise by the Jewish resistance, suffered losses during the first days of the uprising. However, after the period of fighting all over the ghetto, after setting the brush-makers' „shop" in Świętojerska Street afire (a dozen or so Germans died in the rubble), after the major battle waged by the ŻZW at Muranowski Square, the fighters took refuge in underground bunkers which became resistance centres of the embattled ghetto, but the Nazis destroyed them systematically. On May 8th they surrounded the ŻOB command bunker at 18 Miła Street and tossed in a gas-bomb. Choking in the poisonous fumes the members of the command and their comrades took their own lives.

From the first days of the uprising General JŘrgen Stroop, the commander of what was known as the Grossaktion in the ghetto, began a systematic, house after house, burning out of the Jewish district.

After a few days individual fires merged into one sea of flames, and a huge cloud of suffocating smoke hung over the ghetto. It was mainly civilians that died in the flames. Having run out of ammunition and food the decimated ŻOB tried to get out of the burning ghetto in order to continue the struggle in partisan detachments in the woods.

After a few ill-fated attempts some fighters and underground leaders reached the „Aryan side" through sewers with the help of Poles who were members of the PPR and the GL. The first group of some 40 people made it to the „Aryan side" intact on April 29th, but of the group of some 60 people who entered the sewers on May 8th only 30 or so emerged on the surface two days later.

Attempts to evacuate the wounded from the makeshift ŻOB hospital in a bunker at 76 Leszno Street failed. One of the fighters, a charming girl who exuded an air of calm and confidence, volunteered to stay with the patients. In mid-May the Nazis set the bunker afire thus killing the wounded and their guard.

The organizers of the evacuation through the sewers did not manage to get in touch with the remaining three fighting groups. These continued to defend themselves in the ghetto for another few weeks.

On May 16th Stroop gave an order to blow up the synagogue at Tłomackie Street as a sign of the „victory over the Jews". The resistance amidst the ruins of the burnt-out ghetto grew weaker but held out as late as the autumn of 1943.

The last act of the drama of the Warsaw ghetto was played out in the SS camps in the Lublin region: at Trawniki and Poniatowa the Warsaw ghetto deportees organized a ŻOB detachment which apart from conducting mutual aid and cultural activities among the prisoners began to prepare an armed revolt. They did not succeed however. Between November 3rd and 5th, 1943, the Nazis murdered over 25,000 Jews (mainly from Warsaw) at Trawniki, Poniatowa and Majdanek.

The surviving members of the ŻOB once again took to arms against the Nazis during the Warsaw uprising. They fought in the Old Town within the ranks of the AL.

Poles from the AK, GL and other organizations also lost their lives in solidarity actions along the ghetto walls. On the „Aryan side" of the wall the Council for Aid to Jews („Żegota") began to operate in December 1942.

The Polish Jews died in the gas chambers of Chełmno, Bełżec, Sobibór, Treblinka, Auschwitz and Majdanek, in SS labour camps, in the flames of the insurgent ghetto, in sewers and in partisan battles, in armed revolts in other ghettos, and in the Warsaw uprising, and along with them died the ghetto insurrectionaries as well as members of and contributors to the Oneg Shabat. It is thanks to their work, thanks to the archives recovered after the war in the ruins of Warsaw, that from the shapeless and seemingly impersonal human mass treated on the whole only as the object of Nazi atrocities, there emerge full blooded people of high professional and intellectual standing, there emerges a picture of a society of great vitality and creative potential, which bravely and unflinchingly fought for survival.

The ghetto uprising was a struggle against the odds, heroic and tragic. But it was successful in that despite the tragic end, the ghetto fighters fully achieved their two basic objectives: the participation of the Jews from the ghetto in the war against the Nazi Reich became a fait accompli; the other aim which was achieved, and which has had long-term moral repercussions, was to shake the conscience of the world, to protest against genocide.

## ABBREVIATIONS

| | |
|---|---|
| AK (Armia Krajowa) | Home Army |
| AL (Armia Ludowa) | People's Army |
| AZIH (Archiwum Żydowskiego Instytutu Historycznego) | Archives of the Jewish Historical Institute |
| BIP (Biuro Informacji i Propagandy) | Information and Propaganda Bureau |
| Bund | Jewish Socialist Alliance in Poland |
| DR (Delegatura Rządu) | Delegate's Office of the Government |
| GL (Gwardia Ludowa) | People's Guard |
| KK (komisja Koordynacyjna) | Coordinating Committee |
| NSZ (Narodowe Siły Zbrojne) | National Armed Forces |
| PPR (Polska Partia Robotnicza) | Polish Workers' Party |
| PPS (Polska Partia Socjalistyczna) | Polish Socialist Party |
| PS (Polscy Socjaliści) | Polish Socialists |
| WRN (Wolność-Równość-Niepodległość) | Freedom-Equality-Independence |
| ŻIH (Żydowski Instytut Historyczny) | Jewish Historical Institute |
| ŻKK (Żydowska Komisja Koordynacyjna) | Jewish Coordinating Committee |
| ŻKN (Żydowski Komitet Narodowy) | Jewish National Committee |
| ŻOB (Żydowska Organizacja Bojowa) | Jewish Fighting Organization |
| ŻSS (Żydowska Samopomoc Społeczna) | Jewish Mutual Help |
| ŻZW (Żydowski Związek Wojskowy) | Jewish Military Union |

# Re-settlement

# The establishment of a sealed district

# Life in the ghetto

# Forced labour

DIE ZUR ARBEIT HERANGEZOGENEN LEUTE SIND VERPFLICHTET SICH AM BESTIMMTEN TAG PÜNKTLICH UM **6** UHR MORGENS ZU MELDEN

KAŻDY POWOŁANÝ DO PRACY OBOWIĄZANY JEST STAWIĆ SIĘ PUNKTUALNIE O **6** EJ RANO W DNIU WYZNACZONYM

# Terror

# Ecce homo

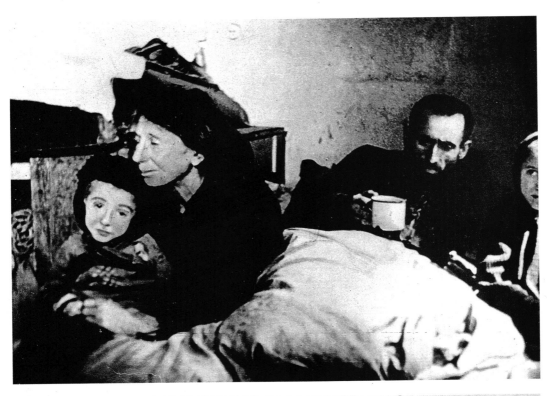

# Children

# Death in
# the ghetto

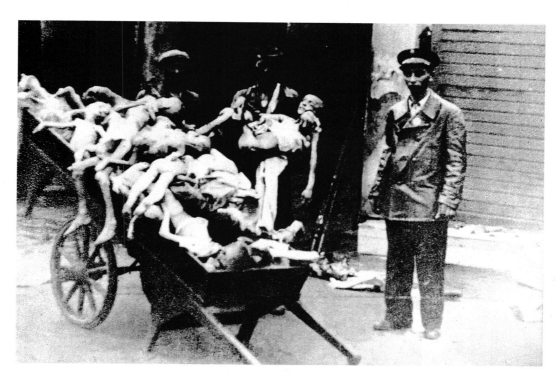

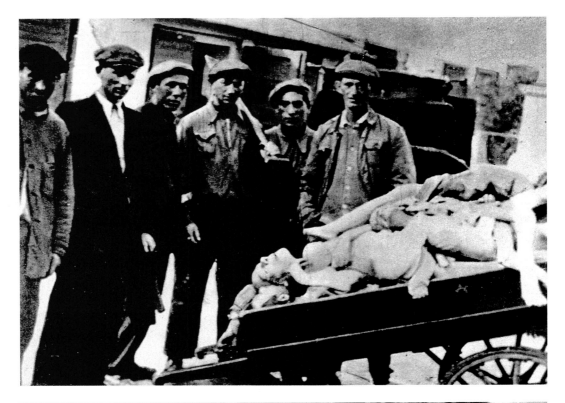

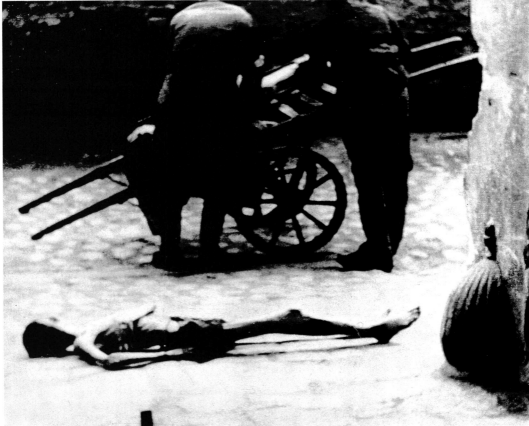

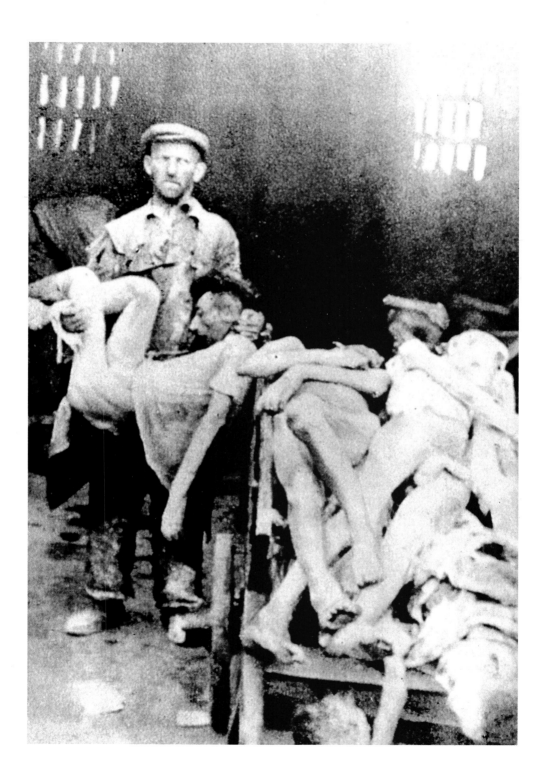

# Deportation

# The uprising

# The last „Deportees"

# From the bunkers and ruins

# Insurgents

# The victors...

# The Warsaw Ghetto 1945

Photographs of the stone desert of the Warsaw Ghetto. It is difficult to recognise which part of the Muranów district is represented in these pictures. Below left – the walls of the Ghetto where the imprisoned Jews rose in arms in the spring of 1943 in a heroic, though uneven, fight against the Nazis. In the front – the watchman's tower from which the German soldiers were hunting for people. Nearby – remnants of prison bars marking the place of the completely destroyed Pawiak prison, one of the many fascist torture places in Warsaw.

Photographs by courtesy of the Central
Commission for the Investigation
of Nazi Crimes in Poland,
Jewish Historical Institute,
Mechanic Documentation Archive and
Documentary Film Studio in Warsaw.
Reproductions of photographs
(„The Warsaw Ghetto", „Warsaw 1945-1948")

Designed and Production by:
RYSZARD NOWICKI
WARSAW, tel.: (022) 635 76 92

Printed in Poland.
Warsaw 1999

Printed and bound by:

DRUKPOL   Warsaw tel. 811-23-43